# WASHINGTON TEST PREP

# Language & Vocabulary

# Student Quiz Book

# Grade 2

ISBN 978-1502968463

# CONTENTS

# INTRODUCTION
# For Parents, Teachers, and Tutors

This workbook will develop all the language skills that students in Washington need. It includes revising and editing exercises that require students to apply language skills, as well as quizzes that focus specifically on each language skill that students are expected to have. This workbook covers the skills listed in the Common Core State Standards.

## Common Core State Standards

The state of Washington has adopted the Common Core State Standards for English Language Arts. These standards describe what students are expected to know, and student learning throughout the year is based on the content of these standards. The standards are divided into the following areas: Reading, Writing, Speaking and Listening, and Language.

This book focuses specifically on developing and applying the Language standards. However, this also overlaps with all other areas, as language skills are essential for effective reading comprehension, speaking, listening, and writing.

## Section 1: Revising and Editing Quizzes

Section 1 of this book focuses on editing and revising. It contains 4 sets of 5 passages. Each passage includes errors or opportunities for improvement. The questions following each passage require students to identify errors that need to be corrected, to identify ways that the passage can be improved, or to apply language skills based on the passage.

This section of the book gives students the opportunity to apply language skills in context. It also meets the Common Core Writing standard that requires students to edit and revise writing based on the content of the Language standards.

## Section 2: Language, Vocabulary, and Grammar Quizzes

Section 2 of this book contains individual quizzes focused on each of the language skills that students need. It covers the skills specifically described in the Common Core Language standards, as well as the skills described in the Foundational Skills of the Reading standards. By focusing on each skill individually, students will gain a full understanding of the skill. As well as developing and improving language skills, this section will enhance reading and writing skills.

# Section 1
# Revising and Editing Quizzes

# Revising and Editing Quizzes

# Set 1

---

### Instructions

Read each passage. Each passage is followed by questions.

For each multiple-choice question, read the question carefully. Then select the best answer. Fill in the circle for the correct answer.

For other types of questions, follow the instructions given.

---

# Building Your Vocabulary

As you read the passages, list any words you do not understand below. Use a dictionary to look up the meaning of the word. Write the meaning of the word below.

Word: _____

Meaning: _____

_____

Word: _____

Meaning: _____

_____

Word: _____

Meaning: _____

_____

Word: _____

Meaning: _____

_____

Word: _____

Meaning: _____

_____

# Quiz 1

## Read the passage below. Then answer the questions that follow it.

### Robot Boy

I'm not a real robot. It's very fun to pretend. My father and I painted a box with silver paint. I glued on bottle tops for buttons. Then my father cut out too holes for my arms. Finally, my father made a large hole to put my head through. I put the box on over my clothes, and I looked just like a real robot.

I enjoy wearing my robot suit outside, in my room, and on the swing. I even weared my robot suit while eating dinner last night. It was hard to get the food in my mouth because I couldn't move my arms easily. I've decided I won't wear my robot suit to dinner anymore.

1  In the passage, the author uses contractions. A contraction is a shortened form of two words. Write the long form of each of the contractions below. The first one has been completed for you.

I'm          _____I am_____

it's          _____

couldn't     _____

I've         _____

won't        _____

**2**    Which word rhymes with *suit*?

    Ⓐ     mate

    Ⓑ     wait

    Ⓒ     hoot

    Ⓓ     truth

**3**    What is the best way to combine the first two sentences?

    Ⓐ     I'm not a real robot, and it's very fun to pretend.

    Ⓑ     I'm not a real robot, for it's very fun to pretend.

    Ⓒ     I'm not a real robot, nor it's very fun to pretend.

    Ⓓ     I'm not a real robot, but it's very fun to pretend.

**4**    Which word should replace *weared* in the sentence below?

    **I even weared my robot suit while eating dinner last night.**

    Ⓐ     wear

    Ⓑ     wore

    Ⓒ     wored

    Ⓓ     wearing

**5**    Which change should be made in the sentence below?

    **Then my father cut out too holes for my arms.**

    Ⓐ     Change *then* to *than*

    Ⓑ     Change *too* to *two*

    Ⓒ     Change *my* to *mine*

    Ⓓ     Change *arms* to *arm's*

# Quiz 2

**Read the passage below. Then answer the questions that follow it.**

## Presidents

In 1789, George Washington became the first president of the United States of America. It is less known that John Adams was the vice president.

John Adams went on to become the second president in 1797. Thomas Jefferson was its vice president.

When John Adams was not any longer president in 1801, Thomas Jefferson became the third president of the United States of America.

George Washington was America's first president. He became president on April 30 1789. He stayed in the role until early 1797.

1    In the word *known*, the letter *k* is silent. For each word below, circle the silent letter in the word. Then write two more words that have the same silent letter.

lamb    _____    _____

ghost    _____    _____

knife    _____    _____

wrong    _____    _____

**2** What is the correct way to punctuate the date below?

&#9398; April, 30 1789

&#9399; April 30, 1789

&#9400; April, 30, 1789

&#9401; April 30 1789

**3** Which is the best way to rewrite the first part of the sentence below?

**When John Adams was not any longer president in 1801, Thomas Jefferson became the third president of the United States of America.**

&#9398; When John Adams was not longer president in 1801,

&#9399; When John Adams was no more president in 1801,

&#9400; When John Adams was not anymore president in 1801,

&#9401; When John Adams was no longer president in 1801,

**4** Which word should replace *its* in the second sentence below?

**John Adams went on to become the second president in 1797. Thomas Jefferson was its vice president.**

&#9398; her

&#9399; his

&#9400; him

&#9401; them

# Quiz 3

**Read the passage below. Then answer the questions that follow it.**

## Neil Armstrong

Neil Armstrong was the ferst man to Walk on the Moon. He did this in 1969 when he was 38 years old. The American space mission he went on was called Apollo 11. It was during this mission that he said the very well known sentence, "One small step for man, one giant leap for mankind."

He has since been in newspapers. He has since been in magazines. He has been on television, and movies have been made about him. He has even been put onto postage stamps. He worked hard and done something great. He is a great role model for people everywhere.

1    Which change should be made in the sentence below?

   **He worked hard and done something great.**

   Ⓐ    Change *worked* to *working*

   Ⓑ    Change *done* to *did*

   Ⓒ    Change *great* to *grate*

   Ⓓ    There is no change needed.

**2**   What is the best way to combine the sentences below?

**He has since been in newspapers. He has since been in magazines.**

Ⓐ   He has since been in newspapers, magazines.

Ⓑ   He has since been in newspapers and magazines.

Ⓒ   He has since been in newspapers and been in magazines.

Ⓓ   He has since been in newspapers, magazines too.

**3**   Which word in the passage should NOT start with a capital letter?

Ⓐ   Armstrong

Ⓑ   Walk

Ⓒ   American

Ⓓ   Apollo

**4**   Which word in the passage is spelled incorrectly?

Ⓐ   ferst

Ⓑ   space

Ⓒ   leap

Ⓓ   movies

**5**   Which word means the opposite of *giant*?

Ⓐ   great

Ⓑ   huge

Ⓒ   brave

Ⓓ   tiny

# Quiz 4

**Read the passage below. Then answer the questions that follow it.**

## Stingrays

Stingrays live in the sea. They are related to sharks, but they look very diffrent. They have a long flat body. They have large flat fins. Each fin looks a bit like a giant wing. They are named for the stinger on their tail. The stingers are pointy and sharp. They contain venom or poison.

Stingrays can hide under a thin layer of sand. Because of this, some people have stepped on a stingray and be stung. However, this is not common. In places where people know there are stingrays, they throw small stones into the water before walking through.

1      The passage describe how stingrays have a "long flat body." The words *long* and *flat* are adjectives, or describing words. Complete each sentence below by adding the adjectives used to describe each object.

A stingray's fins are _____ and _____.

Each fin looks a bit like a wing that is _____.

The stingray's stingers are _____ and _____.

Stingray's hide under a layer of sand that is _____.

**2**   What is the correct way to spell the word *diffrent*?

Ⓐ   difrent

Ⓑ   diferent

Ⓒ   different

Ⓓ   diffarent

**3**   Which two words from the passage rhyme?

Ⓐ   thin, fin

Ⓑ   look, long

Ⓒ   stung, stones

Ⓓ   know, through

**4**   Which change should be made in the sentence below?

**Because of this, some people have stepped on a stingray and be stung.**

Ⓐ   Delete the comma

Ⓑ   Change *stepped* to *stepping*

Ⓒ   Change *be* to *been*

Ⓓ   Change *stung* to *stinged*

**5**   Which word could replace the words "not common"?

Ⓐ   commoner

Ⓑ   commonest

Ⓒ   uncommon

Ⓓ   commonly

# Quiz 5

**Read the passage below. Then answer the questions that follow it.**

## The Missing Button

James was very upset. When Sarah asked him what was wrong, he told her that he had lost a button from his favorite green coat.

Sarah helped James look for the missing button. They looked around the classroom first. They found a button. It was red. The button that James losed was black. James was glad he had a friend to help him search. They finally found the button under the teachers desk.

1    A compound word is a word made by adding together two different words. The word *classroom* is a compound word made up of the words *class* and *room*. For each compound word below, write three more compounds words that end with the same end word.

classroom

_____room      _____room      _____room

baseball

_____ball      _____ball      _____ball

daytime

_____time      _____time      _____time

**2**   Which is the best way to combine the sentences below?

**They found a button. It was red.**

Ⓐ   They found a button, it was red.

Ⓑ   They found a button, so it was red.

Ⓒ   They found a button, but it was red.

Ⓓ   They found a button, then it was red.

**3**   Which word should replace *losed* in the sentence below?

**The button that James losed was black.**

Ⓐ   lose

Ⓑ   losing

Ⓒ   lost

Ⓓ   losted

**4**   Which change should be made in the sentence below?

**They finally found the button under the teachers desk.**

Ⓐ   Change *they* to *them*

Ⓑ   Change *finally* to *final*

Ⓒ   Change *under* to *undder*

Ⓓ   Change *teachers* to *teacher's*

# Revising and Editing Quizzes

## Set 2

### Instructions

Read each passage. Each passage is followed by questions.

For each multiple-choice question, read the question carefully. Then select the best answer. Fill in the circle for the correct answer.

For other types of questions, follow the instructions given.

## Building Your Vocabulary

As you read the passages, list any words you do not understand below. Use a dictionary to look up the meaning of the word. Write the meaning of the word below.

Word: _____

Meaning: _____

_____

Word: _____

Meaning: _____

_____

Word: _____

Meaning: _____

_____

Word: _____

Meaning: _____

_____

Word: _____

Meaning: _____

_____

# Quiz 6

**Read the passage below. Then answer the questions that follow it.**

## A Special Day

Dear Diary,

Today, I gone with my friends to get a library card. I had not ever had a library card before. The librarian asked me to sit in a special seat. Then she took my picture. She printed out a card with my name and my photo on it. Then she used a strange machine to cover the card in plastic. She told me how I could use the card to borrow up to four books.

I am so excited to borrow my first book! I want to find a book that has a superhero in it. There is a lot of books, so I am hopeful that I will be able to find one.

Brin

1    Read this sentence from the passage.

   **I am so excited to borrow my first book!**

   The author ends this sentence with an exclamation mark. Explain whether this is a suitable punctuation mark to use for the sentence.

   _____

   _____

   _____

   _____

**2**    Which word should replace the word *gone* in the first sentence?

Ⓐ    go

Ⓑ    going

Ⓒ    went

Ⓓ    done

**3**    Which word could replace the words "not ever" in the second sentence without changing the meaning of the sentence?

Ⓐ    neither

Ⓑ    never

Ⓒ    always

Ⓓ    almost

**4**    What is the correct way to write the first part of the last sentence?

Ⓐ    There is a lot of book,

Ⓑ    There is a lots of books,

Ⓒ    There are a lot of book,

Ⓓ    There are a lot of books,

**5**    Which word from the passage has the same start sound as *photo*?

Ⓐ    gone

Ⓑ    picture

Ⓒ    borrow

Ⓓ    find

# Quiz 7

**Read the passage below. Then answer the questions that follow it.**

## Soil

 Soil is necessary to grow most plants. It contains the materials that a plant needs to grow. This includes the water that plants need. Some places, such as deserts, may have soil that does not contain everything that a plant needs. This means that plants are not as likeness to live there.

Good soil usually feels moist, not soaking wet. It is commonly a dark brown color. This is due to all of the animals and plants living in it. A lot of food that people eat comes from plants. The plants keep the soil moving. The animals also add food to the soil.

1     The word *desert* is often misspelled *dessert*. Circle the correct spelling of the commonly misspelled word in each sentence below.

The ferry could hold about one hundred peeple / people.

The kitten was very little / littel.

I have a brother and a sister / sisster.

I am looking for my father and muther / mother.

The park is full of happy chilldren / children.

This book is my favorite / favrite.

**2**   Which word should replace the word *likeness* in the sentence below?

**This means that plants are not as likeness to live there.**

Ⓐ   liked

Ⓑ   liking

Ⓒ   likely

Ⓓ   likable

**3**   What is the best way to rewrite the first sentence of the second paragraph?

Ⓐ   Good soil usually feels moist, so not soaking wet.

Ⓑ   Good soil usually feels moist, and not soaking wet.

Ⓒ   Good soil usually feels moist, nor soaking wet.

Ⓓ   Good soil usually feels moist, but not soaking wet.

**4**   Which sentence does NOT belong in the passage?

Ⓐ   *Soil is necessary to grow most plants.*

Ⓑ   *It contains the materials that a plant needs to grow.*

Ⓒ   *It is commonly a dark brown color.*

Ⓓ   *A lot of food that people eat comes from plants.*

**5**   Which word has the same meaning as *necessary*?

Ⓐ   needed

Ⓑ   nice

Ⓒ   likely

Ⓓ   useful

## Quiz 8

**Read the passage below. Then answer the questions that follow it.**

### My Duck Family

I am a duck. I go by the name of Frankie. I live in a pond. The pond is in a park. There are many other ducks. It gets very crowded sometimes.

I have three ducklings named Fuzzy, Feathers, and Fergie. We enjoy swimming around the pond. We love eating bread that the kind humans throw to us. Bread tastes very good. Catching the bread first is a fun game to play with my duck family! We often have to fight other ducks for it as well. It can be hard to get the bread, but it's worth it.

©Jan Mehlich

1   The names of the ducks all start with *f*. Place the names of the ducks in alphabetical order.

   Frankie     Fuzzy      Feathers     Fergie


   _____, _____, _____, _____

**2**   Which meaning of the word *kind* is used in the sentence below?

   **We love eating bread that the kind humans throw to us.**

   Ⓐ   caring and nice

   Ⓑ   a sort or type

   Ⓒ   a group of people

   Ⓓ   in a way


**3**   Which word rhymes with *fight*?

   Ⓐ   fort

   Ⓑ   laugh

   Ⓒ   mist

   Ⓓ   white


**4**   What is the best way to combine the sentences below?

   **I live in a pond. The pond is in a park.**

   Ⓐ   I live in a pond park.

   Ⓑ   I live in a pond in a park.

   Ⓒ   I live in a pond, is in a park.

   Ⓓ   I live in a pond and is in a park.

# Quiz 9

**Read the passage below. Then answer the questions that follow it.**

## Crying Over Onions

It is a well-known fact that chopping onions makes people cry. But why does this happen. There is actually a very good reason for this. It is not because onions make people sad!

Onions contain chemicals. When the onion skin is cut, the chemicals are released into the air. They are released as gases. The gases travel through the air. If the gas gets into your eyes, it causes them to sting. Your body makes you cry to help clean the gas from your eyes. This stops them from stinging. This is one way that the body can help care for itself. The next time your eyes water, don't be annoyed. Be glad that your body is looking after you.

1    The word *chopping* is the base word *chop* with the suffix *-ing* added. When the suffix is added, the *p* is doubled. For each word below, write the word with the suffix *-ing* added to it. Be sure to spell each word correctly.

stop    _____

skip    _____

cut    _____

run    _____

rub    _____

**2**     What is the correct way to end the sentence below?

**But why does this happen.**

Ⓐ     But why does this happen!

Ⓑ     But why does this happen?

Ⓒ     But why does this happen;

Ⓓ     It is correct as it is.

**3**     Read these sentences from the second paragraph.

**Your body makes you cry to help clean the gas from your eyes. This stops them from stinging.**

What does the word *them* in the second sentence refer to?

Ⓐ     the chemicals from the onion

Ⓑ     the person's eyes

Ⓒ     people who cut onions

Ⓓ     the layers of the onion

**4**     Which of these rewrites the last sentence with the most suitable transition word?

Ⓐ     However, be glad that your body is looking after you.

Ⓑ     Finally, be glad that your body is looking after you.

Ⓒ     Instead, be glad that your body is looking after you.

Ⓓ     Also, be glad that your body is looking after you.

# Quiz 10

**Read the passage below. Then answer the questions that follow it.**

## Bones

Bones are a very important part of the body. When a baby human is born, it has over 270 bones. Over time, many of the bones fuse to others. This makes a bone that is more large. Fully grown adult humans have about 206 bones. Bones are made of hard materials. The most important material is calcium.

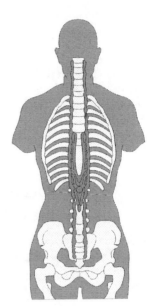

Humans put calcium into their bodies in many ways. One important way is by eating or drinking dairy products like milk and cheese. Calcium is also found in green vegetables like broccoli. Broccoli is easy to grow in a home garden. Calcium is also found in shellfish sardines and almonds. To have healthy bones, make sure your diet includes plenty of calcium.

1    In which sentence does the word *hard* have the same meaning as the sentence below?

**Bones are made of hard materials.**

Ⓐ    The test we took was quite hard.

Ⓑ    I hurt myself when I fell on the hard ground.

Ⓒ    The teacher can be hard on her students.

Ⓓ    It was hard to run to the top of the steep hill.

**2**    What is the best way to rewrite the sentence below?

**This makes a bone that is more large.**

Ⓐ    This makes a larger bone.

Ⓑ    This make a largest bone.

Ⓒ    This makes a more large bone.

Ⓓ    This makes a more larger bone.


**3**    What is the correct way to use commas in the sentence below?

**Calcium is also found in shellfish sardines and almonds.**

Ⓐ    Calcium is also found in shellfish sardines, and almonds.

Ⓑ    Calcium is also found in shellfish, sardines, and almonds.

Ⓒ    Calcium is also found in shellfish sardines, and, almonds.

Ⓓ    Calcium is also found in shellfish, sardines, and, almonds.


**4**    Which sentence does NOT belong in the passage?

Ⓐ    *When a baby human is born, it has over 270 bones.*

Ⓑ    *The most important material is calcium.*

Ⓒ    *One important way is by eating or drinking dairy products like milk and cheese.*

Ⓓ    *Broccoli is easy to grow in a home garden.*

# Revising and Editing Quizzes

# Set 3

---

### Instructions

Read each passage. Each passage is followed by questions.

For each multiple-choice question, read the question carefully. Then select the best answer. Fill in the circle for the correct answer.

For other types of questions, follow the instructions given.

---

## Building Your Vocabulary

As you read the passages, list any words you do not understand below. Use a dictionary to look up the meaning of the word. Write the meaning of the word below.

Word: _____

Meaning: _____

_____

Word: _____

Meaning: _____

_____

Word: _____

Meaning: _____

_____

Word: _____

Meaning: _____

_____

Word: _____

Meaning: _____

_____

# Quiz 11

**Read the passage below. Then answer the questions that follow it.**

## Mother Knows Best

I wanted to eat my dinner in bed.
My mother said, "Eat at the table instead!"
I did not lissen. I should have thought twice.
Now my bedroom is home to two hungry mice!

1   Words that rhyme can have the same letters at the end. The words *twice* and *mice* are an example of this. Other rhyming words have different letters at the end. The words *bed* and *instead* are an example of this. For each set of words below, circle the two words that rhyme. Then write another rhyming word on the blank line.

care        car         chair       cart        _____

hope        cloak       soap        note        _____

rain        ran         plant       plain       _____

wart        start       sort        more        _____

fit         night       write       rate        _____

**2**   Which word from the poem is an adjective, or describing word?

Ⓐ   dinner

Ⓑ   bed

Ⓒ   thought

Ⓓ   hungry

**3**   Which of these is the correct way to spell *lissen*?

Ⓐ   lisen

Ⓑ   lisan

Ⓒ   lissan

Ⓓ   listen

**4**   Which word from the poem is a compound word?

Ⓐ   wanted

Ⓑ   mother

Ⓒ   table

Ⓓ   bedroom

**5**   Which of these is the correct way to shorten "should have"?

Ⓐ   should've

Ⓑ   should'ave

Ⓒ   shouldve'

Ⓓ   shouldave'

# Quiz 12

**Read the passage below. Then answer the questions that follow it.**

## To the Moon

Dear Alex,

(1) I want to be an astronaut I have decided when I grow up. (2) They go up into space! (3) I want to bounce around on the Moon like Neil Armstrong. (4) He was the first person to walk on the Moon. (5) I think it would have been very exciting for him. (6) I think it might also have been a bit scary.

(7) If I left the Earth, I would probably feel scared. (8) I think it would be worth it. (9) I like the idea of looking back at the Earth from space. (10) I hope one day I can become an astronaut. (11) Dad keeps telling me that I will have to do well in math and science. (12) I know I will have to do more better in science.

Bye for now,

Jin

1   Where would be the best place to add the sentence below?

**The Earth would look tiny from space.**

   Ⓐ     After sentence 2

   Ⓑ     After sentence 6

   Ⓒ     After sentence 9

   Ⓓ     After sentence 11

**2**    Which sentence does the art in the passage best relate to?

    Ⓐ    Sentence 7

    Ⓑ    Sentence 9

    Ⓒ    Sentence 10

    Ⓓ    Sentence 11

**3**    Which of these is the best way to combine sentences 5 and 6?

    Ⓐ    I think it would have been very exciting for him, but I think it might also have been a bit scary.

    Ⓑ    I think it would have been very exciting and scary for him.

    Ⓒ    I think it would have been very exciting, and a bit scary too, for him.

    Ⓓ    I think it would have been very exciting for him, but a bit scary as well.

**4**    Which of these is the best way to rewrite sentence 1?

    Ⓐ    I have decided that, when I grow up, I want to be an astronaut.

    Ⓑ    I have decided that I want to be an astronaut when I grow up.

    Ⓒ    When I grow up I have decided that I want to be an astronaut.

    Ⓓ    I want to be when I grow up an astronaut, I have decided.

**5**    Which of these is the best way to rewrite sentence 12?

    Ⓐ    I know I will have to do best in science.

    Ⓑ    I know I will have to do gooder in science.

    Ⓒ    I know I will have to do better in science.

    Ⓓ    I know I will have to do more good in science.

# Quiz 13

**Read the passage below. Then answer the questions that follow it.**

## Animals of the Night

The sun has set. All of the birds is going to sleep. There is no longer the sound of chirping or singing. Many leafs float around. Blow down the city streets. The trees begin to sway in the wind.

Soon, the animals of the night will come out to play. The animals can be very loud. They may call out to each other. They will sometimes find a roof to run across. This sometimes wakes up sleeping humans. They wonder what the sound is above them. Then they drift off to sleep as the animals continue they're play.

1    The words *play* and *sway* both end with the letters *ay*. Choose the pairs of letters that can also be added to the start of *ay* to form a word. Write the words on the lines given.

st    th    cr    tr    bl    sc    cl    gr

_____ay      _____ay      _____ay      _____ay

**2**    Which sentence from the passage is NOT a complete sentence?

Ⓐ    *The sun has set.*

Ⓑ    *Blow down the city streets.*

Ⓒ    *They may call out to each other.*

Ⓓ    *This sometimes wakes up sleeping humans.*

**3**    Which change should be made in the second sentence?

Ⓐ    Change *of* to *off*

Ⓑ    Change *birds* to *bird*

Ⓒ    Change *is* to *are*

Ⓓ    Change *sleep* to *sleeps*

**4**    Which of these is the correct form of the plural of *leaf*?

Ⓐ    leaffs

Ⓑ    leafes

Ⓒ    leavs

Ⓓ    leaves

**5**    Which word should replace the word *they're* in the last sentence?

Ⓐ    there

Ⓑ    their

Ⓒ    they

Ⓓ    them

## Quiz 14

**Read the passage below. Then answer the questions that follow it.**

### Henry the Parrot

My pet is named Henry. Henry is a parrot. He enjoys eating seeds. He enjoys drinking water. When he is fed by my mother, he gets excited and flaps his wings.

One day, he was so excited that he spilled his water all over the floor! Then he stomped around in it. It was very amusing until I had to clean up the mess. Henry is the most great pet that I could ask for.

© Ruth Rogers

1    Complete the table by dividing the words listed below into one-syllable words and two-syllable words.

pet          parrot       enjoys       seeds        water

mother       wings        eating       clean        mess

| One-Syllable Words | Two-Syllable Words |
| --- | --- |
|  |  |
|  |  |
|  |  |
|  |  |
|  |  |

**2**   What is the best way to combine the sentences below?

**He enjoys eating seeds. He enjoys drinking water.**

Ⓐ   He enjoys eating seeds and drinking water.

Ⓑ   He enjoys eating and drinking seeds and water.

Ⓒ   He enjoys eating seeds, drinking water.

Ⓓ   He enjoys eating and drinking, seeds and water.


**3**   Which word or words should replace the words "most great" in the sentence below?

**Henry is the most great pet that I could ask for.**

Ⓐ   greater

Ⓑ   greatest

Ⓒ   more great

Ⓓ   most greatest


**4**   What is the best way to rewrite the first part of the sentence below?

**When he is fed by my mother, he gets excited and flaps his wings.**

Ⓐ   When by my mother he is fed,

Ⓑ   When feeds him my mother,

Ⓒ   When he is by my mother fed,

Ⓓ   When my mother feeds him,

## Quiz 15

**Read the passage below. Then answer the questions that follow it.**

### An Unusual Gift

Alexander Graham Bell was the man who invented the telephone. He was born in scotland in 1847. When Bell was born, he was not given a middle name. Unlike today, most childs did not get a middle name until they were older.

Alexander Bell was 11 years old when a middle name he got. The middle name of "Graham" was given to him as a gift for his 11th birthday. It seems like an unusual gift. It was not that unusual for the time.

1    Which change should be made in the sentence below?

**Unlike today, most childs did not get a middle name until they were older.**

Ⓐ    Change *most* to *more*

Ⓑ    Change *childs* to *children*

Ⓒ    Change *were* to *was*

Ⓓ    There is no change needed.

**2**   What does the prefix in the word *unusual* mean?

   Ⓐ    not

   Ⓑ    more

   Ⓒ    again

   Ⓓ    before

**3**   Which word from the passage should start with a capital letter?

   Ⓐ    Invented

   Ⓑ    Telephone

   Ⓒ    Scotland

   Ⓓ    Today

**4**   Which of these rewrites the last sentence with the most suitable transition word?

   Ⓐ    Again, it was not that unusual for the time.

   Ⓑ    Nearly, it was not that unusual for the time.

   Ⓒ    Finally, it was not that unusual for the time.

   Ⓓ    However, it was not that unusual for the time.

**5**   What is the best way to rewrite the first sentence of paragraph 2?

   Ⓐ    When a middle name he got, Alexander Bell was 11 years old.

   Ⓑ    Alexander Bell, when a middle name he got, was 11 years old.

   Ⓒ    Alexander Bell was 11 years old when he got a middle name.

   Ⓓ    When he got a middle name, 11 years old Alexander Bell was.

# Revising and Editing Quizzes

# Set 4

## Instructions

Read each passage. Each passage is followed by questions.

For each multiple-choice question, read the question carefully. Then select the best answer. Fill in the circle for the correct answer.

For other types of questions, follow the instructions given.

# Building Your Vocabulary

As you read the passages, list any words you do not understand below. Use a dictionary to look up the meaning of the word. Write the meaning of the word below.

Word: _____

Meaning: _____

_____

Word: _____

Meaning: _____

_____

Word: _____

Meaning: _____

_____

Word: _____

Meaning: _____

_____

Word: _____

Meaning: _____

_____

# Quiz 16

**Read the passage below. Then answer the questions that follow it.**

## Turtles

Turtles is the only reptiles that have shells. Turtles use their shells for protection. They pull their heads arms and legs inside of their shell. Most turtles live in fresh water.

Like all reptiles, turtles lay eggs. If a turtle lives mostly on land, it is known as a tortoise. They look different from turtles. They will often be much bigger in size. Turtles can be a lot of fun to watch swim in a pond. Some people even keep turtles as pets.

©Jonathan Zander

1    Which change should be made in the first sentence?

    Ⓐ    Change *is* to *are*

    Ⓑ    Change *that* to *those*

    Ⓒ    Change *have* to *had*

    Ⓓ    There is no change needed.

2    Which word in the sentence below is a verb, or an action word?

    **Most turtles live in fresh water.**

    Ⓐ    turtles

    Ⓑ    live

    Ⓒ    fresh

    Ⓓ    water

**3**   Which sentence would be best to add to the beginning of the passage to state the central idea?

Ⓐ      It is rare to see a turtle.

Ⓑ      There is no need to fear turtles.

Ⓒ      Turtles are interesting animals.

Ⓓ      Turtles eat plants and insects.

**4**   Which of these is a way to rewrite the sentence below without changing the meaning of the sentence?

**They will often be much bigger in size.**

Ⓐ      They will often be much bigger.

Ⓑ      They will be much bigger in size.

Ⓒ      They will often be in size.

Ⓓ      They will often be bigger.

**5**   Which of these shows the correct use of commas in the sentence below?

**They pull their heads arms and legs inside of their shell.**

Ⓐ      They pull, their heads arms and legs, inside of their shell.

Ⓑ      They pull their heads arms and legs, inside of their shell.

Ⓒ      They pull their heads, arms, and legs inside of their shell.

Ⓓ      They pull their heads, arms, and legs, inside of their shell.

# Quiz 17

**Read the passage below. Then answer the questions that follow it.**

## Fish Food

"Come on, it's not that far now!" Sam yelled.

Ben wipe away some sweat and kept going. It was a very warm day, and it just kept getting warmer. Sam and Ben were on their way to the big lake to catch some fish. They had their fishing rods and some bait to put on their hooks.

They finally found a good spot near the lake. They sat down to start fishing. Ben opened the ice cream container where he had asked his mother to put the bait.

"This is not fishing bait. These worms are made of candy!" Ben said. "I should have told Mom I wanted worms to use as bait."

"We could still try," Sam offered. "Maybe the fish will like the candy worms."

Ben wasn't sure it would work. It sounded like fun.

"It's worth a try," Ben said.


1   Rewrite each sentence by placing the quotation marks in the correct place.

    Where are you going? Rachel asked.

    _____

    I am busy right now, Kyra said.

    _____

**2**   What is the correct way to rewrite the second sentence?

   Ⓐ   Ben wiped away some sweat and kept going.

   Ⓑ   Ben wiping away some sweat and kept going.

   Ⓒ   Ben was wiped away some sweat and kept going.

   Ⓓ   Ben will wipe away some sweat and kept going.

**3**   Which change should be made in the sentence below?

   **Sam and Ben were on their way to the big lake to catch some fish.**

   Ⓐ   Change *were* to *where*

   Ⓑ   Change *their* to *there*

   Ⓒ   Change *some* to *sum*

   Ⓓ   There is no change needed.

**4**   Which of these shows the correct word to use when connecting the sentences below?

   **Ben wasn't sure it would work. It sounded like fun.**

   Ⓐ   Ben wasn't sure it would work, so it sounded like fun.

   Ⓑ   Ben wasn't sure it would work, or it sounded like fun.

   Ⓒ   Ben wasn't sure it would work, but it sounded like fun.

   Ⓓ   Ben wasn't sure it would work, and it sounded like fun.

# Quiz 18

## Read the passage below. Then answer the questions that follow it.

### Sports Day

(1) Today is the day my class plays sport. (2) Our teacher asked us which sport we wanted to play. (3) I said I wanted to play football the mostest. (4) My friend Ling said he wanted to play baseball. (5) It seemed like everyone had different ideas.

(6) The teacher asked everyone in the class to choose between football, baseball, and basketball. (7) The teacher added up how many votes there were for each sport. (8) We ended up playing basketball. (9) Our teacher said that it was only fair that we played basketball.

(10) I still wish we could have played football. (11) However, I think it was a fair way to choose. (12) Still fun playing basketball.

1   A compound word is a word made by adding together two different words. The words *football*, *baseball*, and *basketball* are compound words. Each word ends with the word *ball*. For each set below, write three compounds words with the word part shown.

book_____        book_____        book_____

door_____        door_____        door_____

_____man         _____man         _____man

**2**   Where would be the best place to add the sentence below?

**The teacher kept a tally of the votes.**

Ⓐ   Before sentence 6

Ⓑ   After sentence 6

Ⓒ   After sentence 8

Ⓓ   After sentence 9

**3**   Which sentence from the passage is NOT a complete sentence?

Ⓐ   Sentence 1

Ⓑ   Sentence 3

Ⓒ   Sentence 10

Ⓓ   Sentence 12

**4**   Which sentence would best follow sentence 12 to end the passage?

Ⓐ   Our teacher can be hard to talk to.

Ⓑ   I have a lot of friends at school.

Ⓒ   Maybe next time we will play football.

Ⓓ   I am not very good at baseball.

**5**   Which change should be made in sentence 3?

Ⓐ   Change *said* to *says*

Ⓑ   Change *play* to *plays*

Ⓒ   Change *mostest* to *most*

Ⓓ   There is no change needed.

## Quiz 19

**Read the passage below. Then answer the questions that follow it.**

### Basketball

Basketball is a game that have ten players divided into two teams. This means that each team has five players. To play basketball, you bounce a ball and score points by throwing the ball into the basket.

There is a basket at the top of a post on each side of the cort. Each team has a basket to keep safe from the other team. Some people for their career play basketball. Most of those players are above 6 feet tall.

1    In the passage, the word *post* means "a pole." Write another meaning for the word *post* on the lines below.

_____

_____

In the passage, the word *feet* means "a unit of measure." Write another meaning for the word *feet* on the lines below.

_____

_____

**2**    Which change should be made in the first sentence?

   Ⓐ    Change *have* to *has*

   Ⓑ    Change *players* to *player's*

   Ⓒ    Change *two* to *too*

   Ⓓ    There is no change needed.

**3**    What is the correct way to spell *cort*?

   Ⓐ    corte

   Ⓑ    coert

   Ⓒ    coart

   Ⓓ    court

**4**    What is the best way to rewrite the sentence below?

**Some people for their career play basketball.**

   Ⓐ    Some people play basketball for their career.

   Ⓑ    For their career, some people play basketball.

   Ⓒ    Play basketball, some people do, for their career.

   Ⓓ    Do play basketball for their career some people.

**5**    Which word should replace *above* in the last sentence?

   Ⓐ    almost

   Ⓑ    about

   Ⓒ    around

   Ⓓ    over

# Quiz 20

**Read the passage below. Then answer the questions that follow it.**

## Jupiter

Jupiter is the fifth planet from the Sun. It is the largest planet in the Solar System. Jupiter is made up of gases. It does not have a hard crust like the Earth does. This means that there is no solid place for a spaceship or rocket to land. This makes it difficult for scientists to study Jupiter. But scientists have found a way.

Scientists have sent a special camera to study Jupiter. The camera is circling the gas planet. It is in orbit around Jupiter. The camera takes photos of many things. It has taken photos of the sixteen moons around Jupiter.

1    Nouns are words that name people, places, things, or ideas. Proper nouns name a certain person, place, or thing. Proper nouns start with capital letters. Complete the table below by listing three more nouns and three more proper nouns from the passage.

| Nouns | Proper Nouns |
|---|---|
| planet | Jupiter |
|  |  |
|  |  |
|  |  |

**2** Which two words from the passage have about the same meaning?

    Ⓐ    hard, solid

    Ⓑ    gases, crust

    Ⓒ    spaceship, scientists

    Ⓓ    camera, photos

**3** What is the correct way to spell the past tense of *study*?

    Ⓐ    studyed

    Ⓑ    studied

    Ⓒ    studdied

    Ⓓ    studded

**4** What does the word *largest* mean?

    Ⓐ    was large

    Ⓑ    less large

    Ⓒ    more large

    Ⓓ    the most large

**5** What is the correct way to shorten the words "does not"?

    Ⓐ    doesnt

    Ⓑ    does'nt

    Ⓒ    doesn't

    Ⓓ    doesnt'

# Section 2
# Language, Vocabulary, and Grammar Quizzes

## Instructions

For each multiple-choice question, read the question carefully. Then select the best answer. Fill in the circle for the correct answer.

For other types of questions, follow the instructions given.

## Quiz 21: Analyze Words

1    The word *neck* ends in *eck*. Which letter can be added to *eck* to form another word?

    &#9398;    d

    &#9399;    m

    &#9400;    s

    &#9401;    t

2    Which pair of letters can be placed before the letters below to form a word?

          \_\_\_ing

    &#9398;    tw

    &#9399;    sh

    &#9400;    st

    &#9401;    pr

3    Which word rhymes with *sail*?

    &#9398;    will

    &#9399;    school

    &#9400;    while

    &#9401;    male

4    Which word does NOT rhyme with the three other words?

    &#9398;    poor

    &#9399;    war

    &#9400;    store

    &#9401;    car

# Quiz 22: Write and Spell Words Correctly

## Circle the correct way to write the name of the object shown in each picture.

1   bear   bare

2   shepe   sheep

3   bote   boat

4   goat   gote

5   bred   bread

6   plain   plane

7   clock   clok

8   coyn   coin

## Quiz 23: Identify Correct Spellings

**Circle the correct way to write each color below.**

| | | | |
|---|---|---|---|
| **1** | white | wight | whyte |
| **2** | bloo | bleu | blue |
| **3** | grene | green | grean |
| **4** | red | read | rede |

**Circle the correct way to write each fruit below.**

| | | | |
|---|---|---|---|
| **5** | pare | pear | pair |
| **6** | peech | peich | peach |
| **7** | lime | lyme | liem |
| **8** | graip | grape | graep |

**Circle the correct way to write each animal below.**

| | | | | |
|---|---|---|---|---|
| **9** | whail | whale | wale | wail |
| **10** | toad | tode | toed | toade |
| **11** | sele | seel | seal | siel |
| **12** | gouse | gose | goos | goose |

## Quiz 24: Place Words in Alphabetical Order

**1**    Which word would go first in alphabetical order?

Ⓐ    storm

Ⓑ    start

Ⓒ    stir

Ⓓ    string

**2**    Which set of words are in alphabetical order?

Ⓐ    pair, pear, poke

Ⓑ    pair, poke, pear

Ⓒ    poke, pear, pair

Ⓓ    pear, pair, poke

**3**    Using alphabetical order, which word could go between the words?

**clap, _____, clown**

Ⓐ    chop

Ⓑ    clean

Ⓒ    crown

Ⓓ    clue

**4**    List the words below in alphabetical order.

train        three        twist        tiger

_____, _____, _____, _____

## Quiz 25: Divide Words into Syllables

**For each word below, divide the word into two syllables. The first one has been completed for you.**

1   monkey      mon / key

2   before      _____

3   circus      _____

4   happy       _____

5   letter      _____

6   never       _____

7   window      _____

8   yellow      _____

**For each word below, divide the word into three syllables. The first one has been completed for you.**

9   elephant    el / e / phant

10  afternoon   _____

11  family      _____

12  telephone   _____

13  tomorrow    _____

14  wonderful   _____

## Quiz 26: Identify Word Sounds

**1**    **Circle all the words where the "a" sounds the same as in *cat*.**

|        |        |        |        |       |
|--------|--------|--------|--------|-------|
| tag    | apple  | baby   | made   | man   |
| gate   | magic  | splash | whale  | say   |

**2**    **Circle all the words where the "e" sounds the same as in *nest*.**

|        |        |        |        |       |
|--------|--------|--------|--------|-------|
| eat    | bell   | keep   | leg    | fell  |
| feed   | shelf  | tent   | week   | seat  |

**3**    **Circle all the words where the "i" sounds the same as in *kite*.**

|        |        |        |        |       |
|--------|--------|--------|--------|-------|
| nice   | white  | wise   | trip   | still |
| pile   | nine   | life   | fix    | bill  |

**4**    **Circle all the words where the "o" sounds the same as in *stop*.**

|        |        |        |        |       |
|--------|--------|--------|--------|-------|
| block  | bottle | school | bold   | drop  |
| grow   | hole   | dollar | rock   | rope  |

**5**    **Circle all the words where the "u" sounds the same as in *hunt*.**

|        |        |        |        |       |
|--------|--------|--------|--------|-------|
| bush   | button | cute   | thumb  | hurt  |
| lucky  | jump   | push   | use    | such  |

## Quiz 27: Identify and Use Antonyms

1    Which word means the opposite of *tall*?

&#9398;    high

&#9399;    short

&#9400;    big

&#9401;    nice


2    Which word does NOT have the same meaning as the others?

&#9398;    neat

&#9399;    clean

&#9400;    messy

&#9401;    tidy


3    Which word means the opposite of *dark*?

&#9398;    light

&#9399;    nice

&#9400;    dim

&#9401;    scary


4    Which two words have opposite meanings?

&#9398;    bright, idea

&#9399;    rich, great

&#9400;    kind, nasty

&#9401;    wide, broad

## Quiz 28: Use Collective Nouns

**Complete each sentence below by writing the noun that best completes the sentence on the blank line.**

| family | crowd | bunch | team | class |
|--------|-------|-------|------|-------|
| band | pack | forest | pile | row |

1    The _____ waited for the teacher.

2    The _____ played a new song.

3    We walked through the quiet _____.

4    There is a _____ of bananas in the bowl.

5    The _____ enjoyed watching the play.

6    The basketball _____ won the match.

7    Dawn placed her book on top of the _____.

8    The _____ of houses all looked the same.

9    There are four people in my _____.

10    Sam was scared when he saw the _____ of wolves.

## Quiz 29: Use Plurals Correctly

**For each question below, complete each sentence by adding the correct word to the sentence.**

1   We had a _____ in the park.          picnic      picnics

2   I washed all the _____ of the car.      window      windows

3   My house is at the end of the _____.      street      streets

4   I share a _____ with my sister.          room        rooms

5   I drank two _____ of water.          bottle      bottles

6   Sam and I both got new _____.          bike        bikes

7   That_____ is a hundred years old.      clock       clocks

8   There was a huge pile of _____.          leafs       leaves

9   I have a pet _____ named Randy.      mouse       mice

10  They say that cats have nine _____.      lifes       lives

## Quiz 30: Identify Proper Nouns

**Proper nouns start with a capital letter. For each question below, identify the proper noun in the sentence. Then rewrite the sentence with the proper noun capitalized.**

1    Many people like to sleep in on sunday.

_____

2    It rained a lot last june.

_____

3    My sister sarah is older than me.

_____

4    It took hours to get to florida.

_____

5    It would be nice to visit canada one day.

_____

6    These shoes came from walmart.

_____

# Quiz 31: Use Words with Suffixes

**For each question below, select the word that correctly completes the sentence.**

1    The attic was very _____.

    Ⓐ    mess

    Ⓑ    messy

    Ⓒ    messier

    Ⓓ    messiest

2    Trevor _____ walked on the sharp rocks.

    Ⓐ    carefully

    Ⓑ    careful

    Ⓒ    careless

    Ⓓ    caring

3    Skye and Brooke have a strong _____.

    Ⓐ    friendly

    Ⓑ    friends

    Ⓒ    friendship

    Ⓓ    friendless

4    The _____ of the sheep's wool was surprising.

    Ⓐ    softness

    Ⓑ    softer

    Ⓒ    softly

    Ⓓ    soften

## Quiz 32: Spell Commonly Misspelled Words

**For each question below, circle the word in the sentence that is spelled incorrectly. Write the correct spelling of the word on the line.**

1    My favrite time of year is summer.

_____

2    I have only a few close frends.

_____

3    I allways read before going to sleep.

_____

4    Kim sed she wanted to buy a new book.

_____

5    I met some new peeple at school today.

_____

6    It is quite common to be scarred of spiders.

_____

## Quiz 33: Understand and Use Prefixes

**1**    What does the word *restart* mean?

ⓐ    not start

ⓑ    start again

ⓒ    start before

ⓓ    start after

**2**    Which prefix can be added to the word *kind* to make a word meaning "not kind"?

ⓐ    un-

ⓑ    re-

ⓒ    mis-

ⓓ    pre-

**3**    Which prefix should be added to the word to make the sentence correct?

**Phil never eats peas because he __likes them.**

ⓐ    un-

ⓑ    dis-

ⓒ    re-

ⓓ    mis-

**4**    A television that has been *preset* has been

ⓐ    set well

ⓑ    set badly

ⓒ    set after

ⓓ    set before

# Quiz 34: Understand and Use Suffixes

**1**   What does the word *coolest* mean?

    Ⓐ    in a way that is cool

    Ⓑ    the most cool

    Ⓒ    less cool

    Ⓓ    more cool

**2**   Which suffix can be added to the word *hope* to make a word meaning "without hope"?

    Ⓐ    -ful

    Ⓑ    -ing

    Ⓒ    -less

    Ⓓ    -ed

**3**   Which word makes the sentence correct?

**The yellow wall made the room look bright and _____.**

    Ⓐ    coloring

    Ⓑ    colorful

    Ⓒ    colorless

    Ⓓ    colorer

**4**   Which word means "the most nice"?

    Ⓐ    nicer

    Ⓑ    nicest

    Ⓒ    nicely

    Ⓓ    niceness

# Quiz 35: Spell Words with Suffixes Correctly

1    Which underlined word is spelled incorrectly?

    Ⓐ    <u>hopping</u> on one leg

    Ⓑ    <u>jumping</u> up and down

    Ⓒ    <u>joging</u> around the block

    Ⓓ    <u>running</u> down the path

2    Which underlined word is spelled incorrectly?

    Ⓐ    <u>played</u> a game

    Ⓑ    <u>walked</u> home

    Ⓒ    <u>waitted</u> a long time

    Ⓓ    <u>helped</u> a friend

3    Which word is spelled incorrectly?

    Ⓐ    tidyed

    Ⓑ    painted

    Ⓒ    wished

    Ⓓ    skipped

4    Which underlined word is spelled incorrectly?

    Ⓐ    <u>catches</u> a ball

    Ⓑ    <u>sleeps</u> at night

    Ⓒ    <u>watchs</u> the rain

    Ⓓ    <u>counts</u> the coins

## Quiz 36: Use Contractions

A contraction is a shortened form of two words. For example, *I am* can be shortened to *I'm*. For each question below, write the contraction for the two words given. Then write a sentence that uses the contraction.

**1**    you are    _____

_____

**2**    he will    _____

_____

**3**    that is    _____

_____

**4**    is not    _____

_____

**5**    you have    _____

_____

**6**    did not    _____

_____

## Quiz 37: Identify and Use Synonyms

1    Which word means about the same as *shut* in the sentence below?

**The teacher asked Sandy to shut the door.**

Ⓐ    slam

Ⓑ    close

Ⓒ    open

Ⓓ    send

2    Which two words have about the same meaning?

Ⓐ    shiny, dull

Ⓑ    story, tale

Ⓒ    wrap, rap

Ⓓ    cheerful, sad

3    Which word means about the same as *finish*?

Ⓐ    start

Ⓑ    finally

Ⓒ    end

Ⓓ    begin

4    Which word does NOT mean the same as the other three words?

Ⓐ    merry

Ⓑ    sad

Ⓒ    happy

Ⓓ    cheerful

# Quiz 38: Identify Types of Words

**Verbs are action words. Adjectives are describing words. Identify the verb and the adjective in each sentence below.**

1    Harry ran quickly down the road.

Verb _____    Adjective _____

2    We finally won the close game.

Verb _____    Adjective _____

3    I baked a beautiful cake.

Verb _____    Adjective _____

4    Margo washed the dirty clothes.

Verb _____    Adjective _____

5    The dress I bought is too large.

Verb _____    Adjective _____

6    The grass looked green after the rain.

Verb _____    Adjective _____

## Quiz 39: Use Correct Verb Tense

**For each question below, choose the correct verb tense to complete the sentence.**

1    I _____ my story tomorrow.

   Ⓐ    writes

   Ⓑ    wrote

   Ⓒ    was writing

   Ⓓ    will write

2    We _____ ten laps of the pool yesterday.

   Ⓐ    swim

   Ⓑ    swam

   Ⓒ    was swimming

   Ⓓ    will swim

3    Yesterday, I _____ over and hurt myself.

   Ⓐ    trip

   Ⓑ    tripped

   Ⓒ    has tripped

   Ⓓ    will trip

4    I often _____ to school by myself.

   Ⓐ    walk

   Ⓑ    walks

   Ⓒ    was walking

   Ⓓ    has walked

## Quiz 40: Use Pronouns

**For each question below, choose the pronoun that best completes the sentence.**

1   Andrew walked to school by _____.

    (A)    ourselves

    (B)    themselves

    (C)    herself

    (D)    himself

2   I wrote a letter and posted _____.

    (A)    it

    (B)    him

    (C)    her

    (D)    them

3   That dog belongs to me. That is _____ dog.

    (A)    me

    (B)    my

    (C)    mine

    (D)    him

4   The hikers found _____ lost in the woods.

    (A)    herself

    (B)    himself

    (C)    themselves

    (D)    ourselves

# Quiz 41: Understand Shades of Meaning

**For each question below, choose the word that best replaces the underlined words in the sentence.**

1    Gina has only a <u>small number of</u> close friends.

    Ⓐ    some

    Ⓑ    many

    Ⓒ    few

    Ⓓ    little


2    Each puppy in the litter was <u>very very little</u>.

    Ⓐ    short

    Ⓑ    tiny

    Ⓒ    small

    Ⓓ    low


3    The dust blew onto the drying clothes and made them <u>not clean</u>.

    Ⓐ    messy

    Ⓑ    dirty

    Ⓒ    untidy

    Ⓓ    neat


4    Paul <u>ran very fast</u> down the street to try to make the bus.

    Ⓐ    walked

    Ⓑ    jogged

    Ⓒ    trotted

    Ⓓ    raced

## Quiz 42: Understand Word Meanings

1    What does the word *empty* show about the room?

     **Wendy was surprised to see that the room was empty.**

     Ⓐ    It was small.

     Ⓑ    It had nothing in it.

     Ⓒ    It was quiet.

     Ⓓ    It smelled odd.

2    Which word in the sentence tells when the events take place?

     **The chilly evening air made the students shiver.**

     Ⓐ    chilly

     Ⓑ    evening

     Ⓒ    students

     Ⓓ    shiver

3    What does the word *frighten* mean in the sentence below?

     **Joel wanted to sneak up on Carly and frighten her.**

     Ⓐ    wake

     Ⓑ    mean

     Ⓒ    scare

     Ⓓ    shout

## Quiz 43: Spell Words Correctly

**1**    Which underlined word is spelled incorrectly?

Ⓐ    <u>fourth</u> quarter

Ⓑ    feeling <u>angry</u>

Ⓒ    one <u>dollar</u>

Ⓓ    <u>librery</u> book

**2**    Which underlined word is spelled incorrectly?

Ⓐ    <u>major</u> problem

Ⓑ    lemon <u>juice</u>

Ⓒ    <u>magic</u> trick

Ⓓ    large <u>jiant</u>

**3**    Which underlined word is spelled incorrectly?

Ⓐ    <u>twelve</u> months

Ⓑ    <u>middle</u> of the night

Ⓒ    <u>luky</u> number

Ⓓ    <u>bounce</u> the ball

**4**    Which underlined word is spelled incorrectly?

Ⓐ    light as a <u>feather</u>

Ⓑ    in the <u>begginning</u>

Ⓒ    around the <u>corner</u>

Ⓓ    get a second <u>chance</u>

## Quiz 44: Use Correct Punctuation

**1**    Which sentence has correct punctuation?

    Ⓐ    The stars are bright tonight,

    Ⓑ    Do you know what that star is?

    Ⓒ    There is a very cold breeze?

    Ⓓ    Do you like looking up at the stars.

**2**    Which underlined word is written correctly?

    Ⓐ    The <u>cat's</u> always have water.

    Ⓑ    The <u>teacher's</u> desk is new.

    Ⓒ    The <u>shop's</u> are closed tonight.

    Ⓓ    The <u>boy's</u> waited for their bus.

**3**    Which underlined word is written correctly?

    Ⓐ    It <u>is'nt</u> too late.

    Ⓑ    We <u>couldv'e</u> waited longer.

    Ⓒ    They <u>aren't</u> sure what happened.

    Ⓓ    <u>Iv'e</u> never seen her before.

**4**    Complete each sentence by adding one of the punctuation marks below.

.    ?    !

Have you seen Amy anywhere____

We have to go right now_____

It was a long and boring day_____

## Quiz 45: Identify Base Words and Suffixes

**For each question below, write the base word and the suffix on the lines.**

**1** driving

Base word: _____        Suffix: _____

**2** talked

Base word: _____        Suffix: _____

**3** stopped

Base word: _____        Suffix: _____

**4** pulling

Base word: _____        Suffix: _____

**5** makes

Base word: _____        Suffix: _____

**6** smiled

Base word: _____        Suffix: _____

## Quiz 46: Use Homophones

**1**     In which sentence are the underlined words used correctly?

ⓐ     The <u>bare</u> <u>ate</u> a fish.

ⓑ     The <u>bear</u> <u>ate</u> a fish.

ⓒ     The <u>bare</u> <u>eight</u> a fish.

ⓓ     The <u>bear</u> <u>eight</u> a fish.


**2**     In which sentence is the underlined word used correctly?

ⓐ     I like playing baseball <u>to</u>.

ⓑ     I like playing baseball <u>too</u>.

ⓒ     I like playing baseball <u>tow</u>.

ⓓ     I like playing baseball <u>two</u>.


**3**     In which sentence is the underlined word used correctly?

ⓐ     Fiona does not like to <u>were</u> dresses.

ⓑ     Fiona does not like to <u>ware</u> dresses.

ⓒ     Fiona does not like to <u>wear</u> dresses.

ⓓ     Fiona does not like to <u>where</u> dresses.


**4**     In which sentence are the underlined words used correctly?

ⓐ     We were asked to <u>meat</u> near the <u>shoo</u> store.

ⓑ     We were asked to <u>meat</u> near the <u>shoe</u> store.

ⓒ     We were asked to <u>meet</u> near the <u>shoo</u> store.

ⓓ     We were asked to <u>meet</u> near the <u>shoe</u> store.

# Quiz 47: Use Homographs

**Homographs are words that are spelled the same, but have different meanings. For example, the word *bill* can mean "a piece of paper money" or can mean "a beak." For each word below, write two sentences using the word. Use a different meaning of the word in each sentence.**

1    bat   1. _____

                 2. _____

2    park  1. _____

                 2. _____

3    rock  1. _____

                 2. _____

4    wave  1. _____

                 2. _____

5    light  1. _____

                 2. _____

# Quiz 48: Use Correct Subject-Verb Agreement

**For each question below, choose the word that best completes the sentence.**

1  It _____ getting late, so I went to bed.

   Ⓐ    was

   Ⓑ    were

   Ⓒ    is

   Ⓓ    are

2  Jamie _____ too much.

   Ⓐ    talk

   Ⓑ    talks

   Ⓒ    talker

   Ⓓ    talking

3  The dogs _____ playing in the yard.

   Ⓐ    am

   Ⓑ    is

   Ⓒ    was

   Ⓓ    are

4  They _____ to be home before dark.

   Ⓐ    is

   Ⓑ    was

   Ⓒ    has

   Ⓓ    have

# Quiz 49: Analyze Words Based on Root Words

**For each question below, identify the root word. Then use this information to write the meaning of the word. The first one has been completed for you.**

**1**    visitor

      Root word: <u> visit </u>

      Meaning: <u> a person who is visiting </u>

**2**    brighten

      Root word: _____

      Meaning: _____

      _____

**3**    magician

      Root word: _____

      Meaning: _____

      _____

**4**    weekly

      Root word: _____

      Meaning: _____

      _____

## Quiz 50: Apply Words to Real Situations

**1**     List two *machines* you might find in a house.

   1. _____     2. _____

**2**     List two objects that you could describe as *shiny*.

   1. _____     2. _____

**3**     List two words you could use to describe a *city*.

   1. _____     2. _____

**4**     List two objects that are *round*.

   1. _____     2. _____

**5**     List two objects that have *buttons* on them.

   1. _____     2. _____

**6**     Describe two things you could do to *thank* someone.

   1. _____

   2. _____

# Quiz 51: Understand and Use Abbreviations

**Addresses often include abbreviations. Write the correct abbreviation for each address below.**

1    2265 Second Avenue          2265 Second _____

2    180 Main Road               180 Main _____

3    35 Smith Street             35 Smith _____

4    11 Greenway Drive           11 Greenway _____

**Titles used for people are often abbreviated, or written in a shorter form. Write the correct abbreviations for each title below.**

5    William Carter Junior       William Carter _____

6    Mister John Logan           _____ John Logan

7    Doctor Marie Diaz           _____ Marie Diaz

**Write the correct abbreviation for each unit of measure below.**

8    foot            _____

9    yard            _____

10   ounce           _____

11   pound           _____

12   centimeter      _____

## Quiz 52: Understand the Meaning of Compound Words

**Find the compound word described by each clue. Write the word on the line.**

1    the time a person goes to bed    <u>bedtime</u>

2    a cup for putting eggs in    _____

3    a coat you wear in the rain    _____

4    a pen that pigs live in    _____

5    a print made with your foot    _____

6    a pack you wear on your back    _____

**Write the meaning of each compound word below.**

7    weekday    <u>a day during the week</u>

8    fishbowl    _____

9    fingernail    _____

10    playroom    _____

11    snowball    _____

12    hairbrush    _____

# ANSWER KEY

The Common Core State Standards are a set of standards that describe what students are expected to know. Student learning throughout the year is based on these standards. All the exercises and questions in this book cover the Common Core standards.

Each question in Section 1 of this book is based on one language skill described in the standards. The answer key identifies the skill covered by each question. In Section 2, each quiz is focused specifically on one skill listed in the standards. Additional information on the Common Core State Standards is included at the end of the answer key.

# Section 1: Revising and Editing Quizzes

## Set 1

### Quiz 1

| Question | Answer | Language Skill |
|---|---|---|
| 1 | See Below | Use contractions correctly |
| 2 | C | Identify rhyming words |
| 3 | D | Combine sentences correctly |
| 4 | B | Use correct verbs and correct verb tense |
| 5 | B | Use homophones correctly* |

*Homophones are words that are pronounced the same but have different meanings, such as the words *ate* and *eight*.

Q1.  The student should write the following long form of each contraction:
- it is, could not, I have, will not

### Quiz 2

| Question | Answer | Language Skill |
|---|---|---|
| 1 | See Below | Identify and write words with silent letters |
| 2 | B | Use correct punctuation (dates) |
| 3 | D | Revise sentences for clarity and correctness |
| 4 | B | Use pronouns correctly |

Q1.  The student should circle the silent letter indicated below. The student should then write two words that have the same silent letter. Sample answers are given below.
- lam**b**: thumb, bomb, dumb, crumb, limb, debt, doubt, climb
- **gh**ost: whale, school, echo, chord, honest, hour, rhino
- **k**nife: knee, knot, knock, know, knew, kneel, knack
- **w**rong: wreck, wrestle, wrinkle, wrist, write, wrap, sword

**Quiz 3**

| Question | Answer | Language Skill |
|:---:|:---:|:---:|
| 1 | B | Use correct verbs and correct verb tense |
| 2 | B | Combine sentences correctly |
| 3 | B | Use correct capitalization |
| 4 | A | Spell words correctly |
| 5 | D | Identify and use antonyms |

**Quiz 4**

| Question | Answer | Language Skill |
|:---:|:---:|:---:|
| 1 | See Below | Identify and use adjectives |
| 2 | C | Spell words correctly (commonly misspelled words) |
| 3 | A | Identify rhyming words |
| 4 | C | Use correct verbs and correct verb tense |
| 5 | C | Understand and use words with affixes |

Q1.  The student should complete the sentences as listed below:
- A stingray's fins are <u>large</u> and <u>flat</u>.
- Each fin looks a bit like a wing that is <u>giant</u>.
- The stingray's stingers are <u>pointy</u> and <u>sharp</u>.
- Stingray's hide under a layer of sand that is <u>thin</u>.

**Quiz 5**

| Question | Answer | Language Skill |
|:---:|:---:|:---:|
| 1 | See Below | Identify and write compound words |
| 2 | C | Combine sentences correctly |
| 3 | C | Use irregular verbs correctly |
| 4 | D | Use correct punctuation (apostrophes) |

Q1.  The student should list three compounds words ending with the same end word. Sample answers are given below.
- classroom: bedroom, ballroom, bathroom, showroom, sunroom, legroom
- baseball: basketball, football, fastball, fireball, snowball, softball, eyeball
- daytime: bedtime, nighttime, teatime, playtime, overtime, halftime, lifetime

# Set 2

## Quiz 6

| Question | Answer | Language Skill |
|---|---|---|
| 1 | See Below | Use correct punctuation (end punctuation) |
| 2 | C | Use correct verbs and correct verb tense |
| 3 | B | Edit sentences for clarity and correctness |
| 4 | D | Use correct subject-verb agreement |
| 5 | D | Use phonics to identify and compare word sounds |

Q1.   The student should explain that the exclamation mark is suitable. The student may explain that it helps show how excited Brin felt.

## Quiz 7

| Question | Answer | Language Skill |
|---|---|---|
| 1 | See Below | Spell words correctly (commonly misspelled words) |
| 2 | C | Use words with suffixes correctly |
| 3 | D | Revise sentences for clarity and correctness |
| 4 | D | Revise passages for clarity and relevance |
| 5 | A | Identify and use synonyms |

Q1.   The student should circle the following correct spellings: people, little, sister, mother, children, and favorite.

## Quiz 8

| Question | Answer | Language Skill |
|---|---|---|
| 1 | See Below | Place words in alphabetical order |
| 2 | A | Determine the meaning of words with multiple meanings |
| 3 | D | Identify rhyming words |
| 4 | B | Revise sentences for clarity and coherence |

Q1.     The student should list the names in the order below:
  - Feathers, Fergie, Frankie, Fuzzy

## Quiz 9

| Question | Answer | Language Skill |
|---|---|---|
| 1 | See Below | Spell words with suffixes correctly |
| 2 | B | Use correct punctuation (end punctuation) |
| 3 | B | Understand the use of pronouns |
| 4 | C | Use transition words and phrases effectively |

Q1.   The student should write the following words: stopping, skipping, cutting, running, rubbing.

## Quiz 10

| Question | Answer | Language Skill |
|---|---|---|
| 1 | B | Determine the meaning of words with multiple meanings |
| 2 | A | Revise sentences for clarity and coherence |
| 3 | B | Use correct punctuation (commas) |
| 4 | D | Revise passages for clarity and relevance |

# Set 3

## Quiz 11

| Question | Answer | Language Skill |
|----------|--------|----------------|
| 1 | See Below | Identify and write rhyming words |
| 2 | D | Identify different types of words (adjectives) |
| 3 | D | Spell words correctly |
| 4 | D | Identify compound words |
| 5 | A | Use contractions correctly |

Q1. The student should circle the words listed below. The students should then write another rhyming word. Sample answers are given below.

- care, chair: air, bear, wear, stare
- hope, soap: cope, rope, mope, slope
- rain, plain:  brain, cane, main, vein
- wart, sort: short, taught, court, port
- night, write: light, height, white, kite

## Quiz 12

| Question | Answer | Language Skill |
|----------|--------|----------------|
| 1 | C | Revise passages for organization |
| 2 | B | Make connections between passage content and art |
| 3 | D | Combine sentences correctly |
| 4 | B | Revise sentences for clarity and coherence |
| 5 | C | Revise sentences for clarity and correctness |

## Quiz 13

| Question | Answer | Language Skill |
|----------|--------|----------------|
| 1 | See Below | Use phonics to identify words |
| 2 | B | Identify complete and incomplete sentences |
| 3 | C | Use correct subject-verb agreement |
| 4 | D | Use irregular plurals correctly |
| 5 | B | Understand and use homophones* |

*Homophones are words that are pronounced the same but have different meanings, such as the words *ate* and *eight*.

Q1. The student should write the following words: stay, tray, clay, and gray.

**Quiz 14**

| Question | Answer | Language Skill |
|----------|--------|----------------|
| 1 | See Below | Identify the number of syllables in a word |
| 2 | A | Combine sentences correctly |
| 3 | B | Revise sentences for clarity and coherence |
| 4 | D | Revise sentences for clarity and coherence |

Q1.   The student should list the words in the table as below:
- One-syllable words: pet, seeds, wings, clean, mess
- Two-syllable words: parrot, enjoys, water, mother, eating

**Quiz 15**

| Question | Answer | Language Skill |
|----------|--------|----------------|
| 1 | B | Use irregular plurals correctly |
| 2 | A | Understand the meaning of prefixes |
| 3 | C | Use correct capitalization |
| 4 | D | Use transition words effectively |
| 5 | C | Revise sentences for clarity and coherence |

# Set 4

## Quiz 16

| Question | Answer | Language Skill |
|---|---|---|
| 1 | A | Use correct subject-verb agreement |
| 2 | B | Identify different types of words (verbs) |
| 3 | C | Choose a relevant topic sentence |
| 4 | A | Revise sentences for clarity and coherence |
| 5 | C | Use correct punctuation (commas) |

## Quiz 17

| Question | Answer | Language Skill |
|---|---|---|
| 1 | See Below | Use correct punctuation (dialogue) |
| 2 | A | Use correct verbs and correct verb tense |
| 3 | D | Edit sentences for correctness |
| 4 | C | Combine sentences correctly |

Q1.   The student should rewrite the sentences as shown below:
- "Where are you going?" Rachel asked.
- "I am busy right now," Kyra said.

## Quiz 18

| Question | Answer | Language Skill |
|---|---|---|
| 1 | See Below | Identify and write compound words |
| 2 | B | Revise passages for organization |
| 3 | D | Identify complete and incomplete sentences |
| 4 | C | Choose a relevant concluding sentence |
| 5 | C | Edit sentences for correctness |

Q1.   The student should list three compounds words with the word part shown. Sample answers are given below.
- bookmark, bookend, bookcase, bookshop, bookshelf, bookworm
- doorstop, doorknob, doorman, doorway, doorbell, doormat
- fireman, mailman, snowman, workman, handyman, watchman

**Quiz 19**

| Question | Answer | Language Skill |
|---|---|---|
| 1 | See Below | Understand and use homonyms* |
| 2 | A | Use correct subject-verb agreement |
| 3 | D | Spell words correctly |
| 4 | A | Revise sentences for clarity and coherence |
| 5 | D | Revise sentences for clarity and correctness |

*Homonyms are words that have the same spelling and are pronounced the same, but have different meanings.

Q1.  The student should give a meaning of *post* other than "a pole" and a meaning of *feet* other than "a unit of measure." Sample answers are given below.
   - to put something in the mail
   - the part of the body at the end of the leg

**Quiz 20**

| Question | Answer | Language Skill |
|---|---|---|
| 1 | See Below | Identify nouns and proper nouns |
| 2 | A | Identify and use synonyms |
| 3 | B | Spell words with suffixes correctly |
| 4 | D | Understand the meaning of suffixes |
| 5 | C | Use contractions correctly |

Q1.  The student should list any three of the nouns and proper nouns below.
   - Nouns: gases, crust, place, spaceship, rocket, scientists, camera, photos, moons
   - Proper nouns: Sun, Solar System, Earth

# Section 2: Language, Vocabulary, and Grammar Quizzes

**Quiz 21: Analyze Words**

1. A
2. C
3. D
4. D

**Quiz 22: Write and Spell Words Correctly**

| | |
|---|---|
| 1. bear | 2. sheep |
| 3. boat | 4. goat |
| 5. bread | 6. plane |
| 7. clock | 8. coin |

**Quiz 23: Identify Correct Spellings**

| | | |
|---|---|---|
| 1. white | 5. pear | 9. whale |
| 2. blue | 6. peach | 10. toad |
| 3. green | 7. lime | 11. seal |
| 4. red | 8. grape | 12. goose |

**Quiz 24: Place Words in Alphabetical Order**

1. B
2. A
3. B
4. three, tiger, train, twist

**Quiz 25: Divide Words into Syllables**

| | |
|---|---|
| 1. mon / key | 9. el / e / phant |
| 2. be / fore | 10. af / ter / noon |
| 3. cir / cus | 11. fam / i / ly |
| 4. hap / py | 12. tel / e / phone |
| 5. let / ter | 13. to / mor / row |
| 6. nev / er | 14. won / der / ful |
| 7. win / dow | |
| 8. yel / low | |

## Quiz 26: Identify Word Sounds

1. tag, apple, man, magic, splash
2. bell, leg, fell, shelf, tent
3. nice, white, wise, pile, nine, life
4. block, bottle, bold, drop, dollar, rock
5. button, thumb, lucky, jump, such

## Quiz 27: Identify and Use Antonyms

1. B
2. C
3. A
4. C

## Quiz 28: Use Collective Nouns

1. class
2. band
3. forest
4. bunch
5. crowd
6. team
7. pile
8. row
9. family
10. pack

## Quiz 29: Use Plurals Correctly

1. picnic
2. windows
3. street
4. room
5. bottles
6. bikes
7. clock
8. leaves
9. mouse
10. lives

## Quiz 30: Identify Proper Nouns

1. Sunday
2. June
3. Sarah
4. Florida
5. Canada
6. Walmart

## Quiz 31: Use Words with Suffixes

1. B
2. A
3. C
4. A

### Quiz 32: Spell Commonly Misspelled Words
1. favorite
2. friends
3. always
4. said
5. people
6. scared

### Quiz 33: Understand and Use Prefixes
1. B
2. A
3. B
4. D

### Quiz 34: Understand and Use Suffixes
1. B
2. C
3. B
4. B

### Quiz 35: Spell Words with Suffixes Correctly
1. C
2. C
3. A
4. C

### Quiz 36: Use Contractions
Sentences will vary. Any sentence that uses the contraction correctly is acceptable.
1. you're
2. he'll
3. that's
4. isn't
5. you've
6. didn't

### Quiz 37: Identify and Use Synonyms
1. B
2. B
3. C
4. B

**Quiz 38: Identify Types of Words**
1. ran, quickly
2. won, close
3. baked, beautiful
4. washed, dirty
5. bought, large
6. looked, green

**Quiz 39: Use Correct Verb Tense**
1. D
2. B
3. B
4. A

**Quiz 40: Use Pronouns**
1. D
2. A
3. B
4. C

**Quiz 41: Understand Shades of Meaning**
1. C
2. B
3. B
4. D

**Quiz 42: Understand Word Meanings**
1. B
2. B
3. C

**Quiz 43: Spell Words Correctly**
1. D
2. D
3. C
4. B

**Quiz 44: Use Correct Punctuation**
1. B
2. B
3. C
4. ? / ! / .

## Quiz 45: Identify Base Words and Suffixes

1. drive / ing
2. talk / ed
3. stop / ed
4. pull / ing
5. make / s
6. smile / ed

## Quiz 46: Use Homophones

1. B
2. B
3. C
4. D

## Quiz 47: Use Homographs

Answers will vary. Sample answers are given below.
1. I hit the ball with a bat. / The bat flew out of the cave.
2. I played in the park. / My mother tried to park the car.
3. It is fun to dance to rock music. / I threw a rock into the lake.
4. The big ocean wave knocked me over. / It is nice to wave to people you know.
5. The light outside was bright. / The feather was very light.

## Quiz 48: Use Correct Subject-Verb Agreement

1. A
2. B
3. D
4. D

## Quiz 49: Analyze Words Based on Root Words

1. visitor, a person who is visiting
2. bright, make brighter
3. magic, someone who does magic
4. week, every week

## Quiz 50: Apply Words to Real Situations

Answers will vary. Any answers are acceptable provided they show an understanding of the key word in italics. Sample answers are given below.

1. television, computer
2. coin, rock
3. busy, noisy
4. plate, moon
5. coat, telephone
6. write a note, send a present

**Quiz 51: Understand and Use Abbreviations**

1. Ave.
2. Rd.
3. St.
4. Dr.
5. Jr.
6. Mr.
7. Dr.
8. ft
9. yd
10. oz
11. lb
12. cm

**Quiz 52: Understand the Meaning of Compound Words**

1. bedtime
2. eggcup
3. raincoat
4. pigpen
5. footprint
6. backpack
7. a day during the week
8. a bowl that fish live in
9. a nail on your finger
10. a room you play in
11. a ball made out of snow
12. a brush for your hair

# COMMON CORE STATE STANDARDS
# For Parents, Teachers, and Tutors

The Common Core State Standards describe what students are expected to be able to do. Student learning is based on these standards throughout the year. The Common Core standards are divided into the following four areas: Reading, Writing, Speaking and Listening, and Language.

The content of this quiz book is focused mainly on the Language standards. However, parts of the Reading and Writing standards are also covered. The Reading, Writing, and Language standards covered in this quiz book are listed below.

## Reading Standards: Foundational Skills

*The Foundational Skills listed as part of the Reading standards describe the basic conventions of English that students need to read and comprehend texts. These skills are covered by some of the questions in Section 1 of this book and by some of the quizzes in Section 2 of this book. The standards covered are listed below.*

**Know and apply grade-level phonics and word analysis skills in decoding words.**
a. Distinguish long and short vowels when reading regularly spelled one-syllable words.
b. Know spelling-sound correspondences for additional common vowel teams.
c. Decode regularly spelled two-syllable words with long vowels.
d. Decode words with common prefixes and suffixes.
e. Identify words with inconsistent but common spelling-sound correspondences.
f. Recognize and read grade-appropriate irregularly spelled words.

**Read with sufficient accuracy and fluency to support comprehension.**
a. Read on-level text with purpose and understanding.
b. Read on-level text orally with accuracy, appropriate rate, and expression on successive readings.
c. Use context to confirm or self-correct word recognition and understanding, rereading as necessary.

## Writing Standards

*The Writing standards describe the production of writing, as well as the editing and revising of writing. The questions in Section 1 of this book cover the editing and revising standard below.*

With guidance and support from adults and peers, focus on a topic and strengthen writing as needed by revising and editing.

# Language Standards

*The Language standards describe the grammar, language, and vocabulary skills expected of students. The questions in Section 1 of this book require students to apply these skills, while the quizzes in Section 2 focus specifically on developing and improving these skills. The Language standards are listed below.*

**Demonstrate command of the conventions of standard English grammar and usage when writing or speaking.**
a. Use collective nouns.
b. Form and use frequently occurring irregular plural nouns.
c. Use reflexive pronouns (e.g., myself, ourselves).
d. Form and use the past tense of frequently occurring irregular verbs.
e. Use adjectives and adverbs, and choose between them depending on what is to be modified.
f. Produce, expand, and rearrange complete simple and compound sentences.

**Demonstrate command of the conventions of standard English capitalization, punctuation, and spelling when writing.**
a. Capitalize holidays, product names, and geographic names.
b. Use commas in greetings and closings of letters.
c. Use an apostrophe to form contractions and frequently occurring possessives.
d. Generalize learned spelling patterns when writing words.
e. Consult reference materials, including beginning dictionaries, as needed to check and correct spellings.

**Use knowledge of language and its conventions when writing, speaking, reading, or listening.**
a. Compare formal and informal uses of English.

**Determine or clarify the meaning of unknown and multiple-meaning words and phrases based on grade 2 reading and content, choosing flexibly from an array of strategies.**
a. Use sentence-level context as a clue to the meaning of a word or phrase.
b. Determine the meaning of the new word formed when a known prefix is added to a known word.
c. Use a known root word as a clue to the meaning of an unknown word with the same root.
d. Use knowledge of the meaning of individual words to predict the meaning of compound words.
e. Use glossaries and beginning dictionaries, both print and digital, to determine or clarify the meaning of words and phrases.

**Demonstrate understanding of word relationships and nuances in word meanings.**
a. Identify real-life connections between words and their use (e.g., describe foods that are *spicy* or *juicy*).
b. Distinguish shades of meaning among closely related verbs (e.g., *toss, throw, hurl*) and closely related adjectives (e.g., *thin, slender, skinny, scrawny*).

**Use words and phrases acquired through conversations, reading and being read to, and responding to texts, including using adjectives and adverbs to describe.**

# Take language skills to the next level with the Common Core Language series.

With exercises that progress from easy to advanced, students will build their skills and enhance language and vocabulary skills to exceed grade level expectations.

There are four books available based on the key Common Core skills most requested by teachers and parents.

Made in the USA
San Bernardino, CA
07 March 2016